Inventions That Shaped the World

The Printing PRESS

ANN HEINRICHS

Franklin Watts
A Division of Scholastic Inc.
New York • Toronto • London • Auckland • Sydney
Mexico City • New Delhi • Hong Kong
Danbury, Connecticut

Photographs © 2005: Art Resource, NY: 23 (Bildarchiv Preussischer Kulturbesitz), 11, 21, 48 (Erich Lessing), 25 (Scala/HIP), 19 (Victoria & Albert Museum, London); Corbis Images: 18 (Archivo Iconografico, S.A.), cover bottom left (Austrian Archives), cover top left, 7, 14, 30, 33, 37, 42, 57, 58, 61, timeline background (Bettmann), 56 (E.O. Hoppé), chapter openers, 38 bottom, timeline spots (Jacqui Hurst), 67 (Gabe Palmer), 54 (Royalty-Free), 16 (Sandro Vannini); Corbis Sygma: 64 (Bernard Annebicque), 51 (Regis Bossu); Getty Images: 62 (London Express), cover bottom right (Photodisc Green); Index Stock Imagery/Erin Garvey: cover top right; Lucidity Information Design: 44; North Wind Picture Archives: 5, 32, 38 top, 60; PictureQuest/Photodisc: 40, 53; Stock Montage, Inc.: 9; Stone/Getty Images/Ken Whitmore: cover center right; The Art Archive/Picture Desk: 8 (The Bodleian Library, Oxford), 12 (The British Library), 43 (Galleria d'Arte Moderna Rome/Dagli Orti), 28 (Musee des Beaux Arts Grenoble/Dagli Orti); The Image Works/Christopher Fitzgerald: 66.

Cover design by Robert O'Brien
Book production by Tricia Griffiths Swatko

Library of Congress Cataloging-in-Publication Data

Heinrichs, Ann.
   The printing press / Ann Heinrichs.
     p. cm. — (Inventions that shaped the world)
   Includes bibliographical references and index.
   ISBN 0-531-12343-X (lib. bdg.)   ISBN 0-531-16722-4 (pbk.)
  1. Printing—History—Juvenile literature. 2. Printing presses—History—Juvenile literature. I. Title. II. Series.
         Z124.H47 2004
         686.2'09—dc22   2004001672

CONTENTS

CHAPTER ONE

The Need to Read

"I cannot live without books."
—Thomas Jefferson, 1815

Imagine how life would be if no one had anything to read. You would never have heard of China or dinosaurs or outer space.

No one would know what was happening in other parts of the world.

That's what it was like before type and the printing press. People knew very little about the world beyond their own villages. For children and adults alike, there was no

Handwritten and illustrated books were owned only by nobles and church officials.

5

such thing as curling up with a good book to read. Books were handmade, one by one. Only religious communities and high-ranking nobles owned them. Books were so precious that they were often locked away or even chained to walls.

The printing press changed all that. Johannes Gutenberg, a German metalworker, dreamed of putting books into the hands of almost everyone. He invented the printing press—a mechanical printing machine that could mass-produce books.

The key innovation in Gutenberg's printing press that allowed him to make books with speed was *movable type.* That is, each letter on a page was printed from a letter cast from a separate piece of metal. When you think of all the letters in a whole book, this sounds like a long and tiresome process. But Gutenberg saw it as the most efficient method to use, and he was right. Separating the letters paved the way for today's keyboard typing and high-technology printing.

Human Hands at Work

The year 1455 is usually considered the date Gutenberg's press was invented. That was the year he completed his landmark printing project—a magnificent Bible. In spite of his achievement, Gutenberg was not famous during his lifetime. He was scarcely known beyond his hometown. In fact, it was not until the late 1700s that scholars pinpointed Gutenberg as the inventor of the printing press.

Actually, some kinds of printing existed long before Gutenberg's time. The Chinese had been printing with hand-carved woodblocks for centuries. They carved each page into wood, brushed the wood with ink, and pressed paper against it.

In Gutenberg's lifetime, some books were printed with woodblocks. But most were handwritten. A scribe, or expert writer, dipped a goose quill into glossy black ink and wrote the words out by hand, carefully forming each letter. Artists added beautifully colored pictures and fancy borders. Gutenberg dreamed of printing books that were just as beautiful as these handcrafted works of art but in less time.

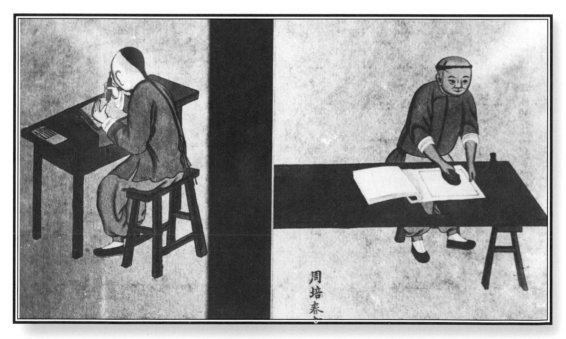

Chinese woodcutters (left) carved impressions into blocks of wood. The printer (right) inked the block and pressed paper against it.

This manuscript page was handwritten by a scribe. An artist then illustrated the border with a flora-and-fauna design.

Rebirth and Revolution

The printing press came along at an exciting time in history. The Middle Ages, or medieval times, were coming to an end. This period was a time of looking inward toward spiritual concerns. Around 1400, a period called the Renaissance, which means "rebirth," began. In the Renaissance, people awakened to new ways of thinking. They began to look at the world in fresh, new ways. They looked outward toward nature and human affairs. Sciences such as medicine, chemistry, and astronomy flourished. Explorers sailed the oceans and discovered new lands.

The printing press was part of this revolution. People wanted to read more than just the Bible and other religious texts. They wanted to read about history and faraway places. They wanted to learn about new scientific ideas. Thanks to the printing press, all this new information could spread quickly.

During the Renaissance, people craved to learn. The printing press allowed for new information to spread far and wide.

9

The Master Problem Solver

Some people say that Gutenberg didn't invent anything new. He just took techniques that already existed and put them together in a new way. Yet, Gutenberg's invention was an astounding feat of imagination and technical skill.

Have you ever had a big problem to solve? Maybe that problem rolled around in your head for hours, or even for days or weeks. That's how it was for Gutenberg. He imagined producing a great number of books in a short time. Yet, bookmaking in his time was a slow, painstaking process. It could take months or years to make just one book.

Gutenberg broke this problem down into many separate parts. Handwriting and woodblock printing were too slow. Inks were too runny. Wood and even metal were too soft to use as type for high-volume printing. Pressing paper against letters by hand was too sloppy and time-consuming.

Gutenberg puzzled over each of these problems. One by one, he found ways to solve them. He brought together ideas from many different areas—even from the craft of wine making! Some problems took years to solve. But Gutenberg was single-minded and kept his goal in sight. Once he succeeded, he changed our world forever.

CHAPTER TWO

Printing: An Ancient Art

As early as 3000 B.C., printing was practiced by the Sumerians of Mesopotamia, in present-day Iraq. They carved words and designs into stone and then pressed the stones onto clay tablets. Other ancient peoples used wood blocks to print designs onto cloth.

The Chinese were printing with woodblocks by the fifth century A.D. They carved a full page of text and

This Sumerian tablet is a bill of sale for a field and one house.

11

pictures onto a block of wood. Everything was carved in relief—that is, sticking up from the background. This raised-up image was the surface that would print.

Each page was also carved backwards. If you've ever used a rubber stamp, you know why. When you look at the stamp's surface, you see that the image is backwards. When you press it onto an ink pad and stamp it onto paper, the image is reversed and looks right.

For centuries, block printing was a technique used in the Far East. The Diamond Sutra *displays the talent and skill of its block cutter.*

Chinese woodblocks worked the same way. The printer brushed ink across the backwards image, laid paper over it, and pressed. When the paper was removed, it was a right-reading page. The Chinese used this system to make the first-known printed book—the *Diamond Sutra*. This religious text was printed in A.D. 868.

Movable Type

Traditionally, we honor Gutenberg for inventing movable type. Instead of creating a whole page in one block, he made a single piece of type for each letter. Actually, however, the Chinese began using movable type about four hundred years earlier than Gutenberg did. The Chinese scientist Pi Sheng invented this system around 1041.

To get an idea of what a huge project this was, take a look at the Chinese writing system. Our Western alphabet has twenty-six letters, but Chinese and many other Asian languages have thousands of characters. Each one is an ideogram—a stylized picture that conveys an idea.

Pi Sheng mixed clay with glue, shaped it into separate Chinese characters, and let them dry. Then he lined up rows of characters on an iron plate, inked them, and pressed paper against them. Once the printing was done, Pi Sheng could re-sort the characters and use them again.

Other Asian craftspeople would print with movable type. They all faced a serious drawback, though—the sheer

In the eleventh century, Pi Sheng invented movable, reusable type.

number of characters. In the 1300s, one Chinese official had a servant carve more than 60,000 characters from wood. A century later, King Htai Tjong of Korea had 100,000 characters cast in bronze. As you can imagine, this method was not practical for making large quantities of books.

The Paper Trail

Many Chinese products and inventions reached Europe along trade routes. Silk, tea, porcelain pottery, and gunpowder are just a few examples. Traders' camels, laden with goods, crossed hundreds of miles of desert and mountain from China to European markets. The art of movable-type printing never made that journey, but another invention did—paper.

The Chinese invented paper around A.D. 105. Before then, they had been writing on silk cloth, but paper made a much better writing surface. Papermaking quickly spread throughout China and neighboring lands.

Through Arab traders, paper reached Baghdad (now in Iraq) in the 700s. Another four hundred years passed before the secrets of papermaking reached Europe. By the 1300s, both Italy and Germany had water-powered mills. More mills sprung up throughout Europe. This was a big step in setting the stage for the printing press.

THE HISTORY OF PAPER

Where does the word *paper* come from? It comes from the name of papyrus, a plant that grows in the marshes along Egypt's Nile River. Ancient Egyptians were using papyrus as a writing material as early as 3500 B.C. (below).

Egyptians took the soft, spongy material inside the papyrus stalk and cut it into many thin strips. They arranged these strips in a crosshatch pattern—alternating vertical and horizontal strips—to form a sheet. The sheet was moistened, pressed, and dried in the sun. Several sheets were then pasted together so they could be rolled up as a scroll.

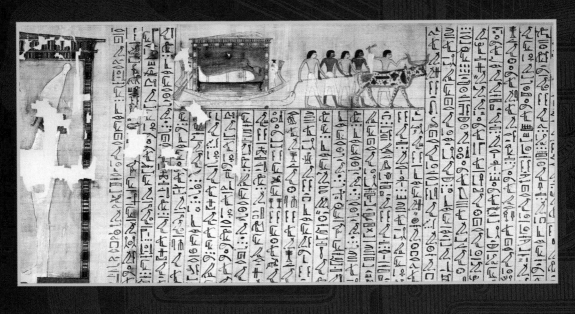

16

Papyrus was the main writing material in the ancient world. It spread from Egypt to the Greek and Roman empires. In the Middle Ages Europeans were not entirely pleased with papyrus. With its coarse plant fibers, it was not smooth enough for fine handwriting. Papyrus also became brittle and often cracked when rolled up. Scribes preferred to write on *parchment* and *vellum*, which were made from animal skins.

Around A.D. 105, a Chinese court official named Ts'ai Lun made paper from mulberry tree bark, hemp fibers, cloth rags, and fishnets. He soaked the materials in water, mashed them into a *pulp*, and pressed the pulp into sheets.

Europeans used Ts'ai Lun's same techniques, making paper from cotton and linen rags. In the 1800s, wood replaced rags as the major pulp source. The wood was ground up and "cooked" to make pulp. The pulp was beaten until smooth, pressed into sheets, and dried.

Today, some paper is still made from cotton and linen scraps. Called rag paper, it is strong, attractive, and long-lasting. Paper money, elegant stationery, and fine-art prints are all made with rag paper. However, most paper is made from wood pulp. As people become more concerned about disappearing forest lands, recycled wastepaper is a growing pulp source.

Manuscripts: The Art of the Scribe

Even without printing presses, Europeans were making books. In religious communities called monasteries and convents, monks and nuns carefully wrote out the Bible and other religious texts by hand. The scribes either copied from another book or wrote as a reader recited the text aloud. The scribe used a goose quill with its tip cut at a slanted angle to write, which put a graceful angle on the beginning and ending strokes of each letter.

These manuscripts, or handwritten books, were beautifully decorated. Pictures, fancy capital letters, and border designs were added with gold or silver and brilliantly colored inks. Different ink colors were made from minerals or plants ground to powder and mixed with a paste. The designs seemed to glisten with light. These books are called illuminated manuscripts.

Scribes wrote on vellum, a fine animal skin. Even after paper was available, most scribes still used vellum. Paper was considered too flimsy to hold up under so much ink.

Monks and nuns worked as scribes.

ILLUMINATED MANUSCRIPTS

The art of creating illuminated manuscripts reached its height during the late Middle Ages. Monastery and convent libraries held thousands of these precious books.

It took many specialized skills to create an illuminated manuscript. Scribes produced the beautiful lettering. Illuminators added gold and other shiny metals. Flourishers drew curlicues of flowers, leaves, and vines. Miniaturists painted tiny figures and scenes. These artistic details were not just decorations. They taught spiritual lessons and lifted the reader's mind and heart toward God.

Besides the Bible the most common illuminated manuscript was a Book of Hours. This was a prayer book that followed the cycle of prayer in monasteries and convents. It divided the day into eight parts, or hours, each with its special prayers. Each feast day of the religious calendar had its own set of prayers.

Books of Hours (left) began as prayer books for monasteries and convents. By the early 1400s, they were being used for private devotion by wealthy nobles who could afford to buy them. The demand for Books of Hours was so high that workshops opened in France, Belgium, and Germany to produce them. Some nobles even employed manuscript artists in their households. A family treasured its Book of Hours and passed it down for generations.

Woodblock Printing in Europe

By the late 1300s, Europeans were printing with woodblocks. The skilled craftspeople who carved the wood were called engravers. They used a knife and chisel to cut letters and pictures into the blocks of wood.

At first, woodblocks were used only to make pictures and fancy capital letters for handwritten manuscripts. After a scribe had finished copying a page of text, the woodblock elements were stamped onto the page. Later, engravers began carving entire book pages from wood.

It took a lot of time to carve out a page—and remember, the whole page was carved backwards, reading from right to left. Often it wasn't worth the trouble. A good scribe

UNIVERSITIES AND SCHOOLBOOKS

In the early Middle Ages, most books in Europe were religious books. Likewise, getting an education meant getting a religious education. That began to change as European society became more complex. Students needed to be trained for specialized professions, such as medicine and law. This need led to the creation of the first universities.

Many of Europe's major cities began opening universities in the 1100s and 1200s. They taught both religious and secular (nonreligious) subjects. University students needed books, and those books were still written out by hand. Professional scribes copied them in scriptoria, or writing shops. The scriptoria also produced religious texts for wealthy nobles.

could write out the same page in much less time. Therefore, woodblock printing was used mostly for one-page items that were in high demand. Prayers, religious pictures, and playing cards were commonly printed with woodblocks.

Gutenberg: In the Right Place at the Right Time

Gutenberg could see the growing need for printed material. He lived in a time when a new social class was emerging in Europe. For centuries there had been two major social

In this 1539 painting, a tenant couple brings their rent to the tax collector whose open book shows their lease agreement.

classes. At the top were wealthy nobles and church officials. At the bottom were peasant farmers. However, as trade increased, a new middle class arose. It consisted of merchants who sold goods and tradespeople who provided services. These people needed printed documents in their businesses.

At the same time the need for books was greater than ever. The new middle class could afford to buy books for their personal libraries. Of course, they wanted Bibles and prayer books, but they also wanted secular books. They were curious about geography, history, astronomy, and the worlds of knowledge beyond their own experiences.

Clearly, scribes could not keep up with the demand for books. Woodblock printers were no more efficient. Gutenberg dreamed of producing a great quantity of books— and fast. Though he would meet with many disappointments, he turned his dreams into reality.

CHAPTER THREE

The Man Who Changed the World

Johannes Gutenberg's full name was Johann Gensfleisch Zur Laden Zum Gutenberg. He was born around the year 1400 in Mainz, Germany. Johannes's father was a patrician—a member of society's upper class. He owned a large estate, with farmland and several houses for the farm workers' families.

Johannes's father and uncle were officers in Mainz's mint, which made coins. As a child,

Johannes Gutenberg, inventor of the printing press

Johannes may have watched the coin makers at work. They carved patterns into steel, stamped the image into a *mold*, and melted metal to pour inside. Johannes himself would practice all these skills as an adult.

Many details of Gutenberg's early life are rather sketchy. Like most patrician boys, he probably attended a Latin school. Latin was the language of scholars and of the Roman Catholic Church. Knowing Latin was the mark of a well-educated, upper-class gentleman.

WHEN WAS HE BORN?

No one knows exactly when Johannes Gutenberg was born. Various documents suggest sometime between 1393 and 1403. In 1900, through an international agreement, scholars decided to consider 1400 as his year of birth.

Patricians, Merchants, and Guilds

Below the patrician class were merchants and craft workers. Most craftspeople belonged to organizations called craft *guilds*. Merchants and guilds could be powerful forces in a city. After all, they controlled the city's economic life. They sometimes clashed with the patricians for power. A typical conflict involved who should pay taxes and who should collect them.

That's what happened in Mainz in 1411. More than a hundred patricians left the city, including the Gutenbergs. They moved to the town of Eltville. It is likely that Johannes went on to study at the nearby University of Erfurt. The Gutenbergs eventually moved back to Mainz, but the guilds took control of the city around 1428. Johannes, now an adult, fled to the city of Strassburg.

Even though he came from a patrician family, Gutenberg had some skills in goldsmithing and jewel cutting. Records show that he taught these skills to pupils in Strassburg around 1437. Gutenberg also practiced a craft that had a direct link to his later inventions—metalworking.

Craft workers at a goldsmith's guild

MEDIEVAL CRAFT GUILDS

Craft guilds were an early type of manufacturing organization. One city might have a stonecutters' guild, a goldsmiths' guild, a shoemakers' guild, and so on.

The first guilds were small, family-owned workshops. Each workshop became like a factory. Its workers produced large quantities of things that were alike in design.

A master craftsperson owned the workshop and trained *apprentices* in the skills of his craft. Most apprentices were preteen or teenage boys who lived in the master's household. They received no wages. In fact, their parents paid the master a hefty sum for their training.

After working for several years as an apprentice, a worker moved up to the level of *journeyman*. Then he could journey, or work for other masters, and be paid for his labor.

In his spare time a journeyman might work on his "masterpiece"—a grand work that showed off his finest skills. The guild's master craftspeople inspected the masterpiece carefully. If they were satisfied, they voted to accept the journeyman as a master craftsperson. This system also made sure that products met high standards of quality.

A few guilds admitted women, such as butchers' and bakers' guilds. Female apprentices trained under the master's wife. Some crafts, such as spinning, were almost exclusively performed by women. Many women worked with their husbands, practicing the same craft alongside them. However, a woman was rarely accepted as a master unless she was continuing her husband's business after his death.

Hot Metal and Pilgrims' Dreams

Every seven years thousands of pilgrims traveled to the city of Aachen, northwest of Mainz. They gathered at Aachen's cathedral to gaze upon precious relics. These relics were articles of clothing believed to have been worn by the Holy Family—Jesus, Mary, and Joseph. (The relics of Aachen are still displayed every seven years.) In Gutenberg's time the pilgrims took mirrors with them to "absorb" blessings from the relics. They hoped to capture the relics' spiritual power and use it to benefit loved ones back home.

Gutenberg knew that 1440 would be a pilgrimage year. So did other Strassburg investors and craftspeople. They formed a cooperative organization to manufacture these "pilgrim mirrors." The mirrors were set into a decorative metal frame made of an **alloy** of lead and tin. The metal was cast—that is, it was melted and poured into a mold. Later, Gutenberg would develop a similar alloy to make blocks of metal type.

Gutenberg's Secret

Meanwhile, Gutenberg was hard at work on a project of his own. He convinced several men to lend him money—but what was it for? Gutenberg wouldn't tell. He insisted on keeping it a secret. But the lenders needed to know they'd get their money back. They insisted that they be partners in

In his workshop, Gutenberg secretly worked on his printing press.

the project, too. Gutenberg had no choice. In 1438, he entered into a five-year contract with three men.

Later that year one of the partners, Andreas Dritzehn, died. Then the Dritzehn family wanted to be partners, and they wanted in on the secret. They sued Gutenberg, and a trial was held.

Witnesses at the trial revealed some details about Gutenberg's secret project. A goldsmith had sold him printing supplies. A carpenter knew Gutenberg was building a wooden press. Clearly, some kind of invention was taking place. But the Dritzehns would never learn what it was, because they lost the lawsuit.

Financing the Vision

By 1448, Gutenberg was back in Mainz. There he borrowed money from his brother-in-law. It is believed that Gutenberg had a printing workshop in Mainz. There he kept tinkering with methods and materials for his printing press.

Meanwhile, to keep money flowing in, he printed things in high demand, such as Latin grammar schoolbooks and indulgence letters. Indulgences were assurances that sins would be forgiven if certain prayers and devotions were offered. The church sold indulgences to raise money for wars in the Holy Land.

By 1450, Gutenberg was close to perfecting his printing system. He paid a visit to a wealthy Mainz goldsmith named

Gutenberg shows proofs produced from movable type to investor Johann Fust.

Johann Fust. Gutenberg must have revealed something about his invention to Fust, because he was able to coax a good deal of money out of him. Fust lent him 800 guilders. That was quite a lot of money in those days. An average worker earned about 10 guilders in a whole year.

Two years later Gutenberg enticed another 800 guilders from Fust. This time, though, Fust expected something in return. In exchange for the loan, he insisted on being granted a partnership in Gutenberg's project.

Losing It All

Time passed, and Fust grew impatient. He expected to make a lot of money from Gutenberg's invention, and it just wasn't happening fast enough. Meanwhile, Gutenberg worked on perfecting every detail of his printing method. By his side was his skilled apprentice, Peter Schöffer.

By 1455, Gutenberg was almost finished printing his first two books. The first would be his masterpiece—a Bible. The other was a Psalter, or prayerbook of Psalms. But Fust was tired of waiting for his money. In November 1455, he sued Gutenberg. He demanded his 1,600 guilders, plus interest— a total of 2,026 guilders.

Fust won his lawsuit, and Gutenberg was crushed. Financially, this wiped him out. There was no way he could pay back the money. He had spent it all on equipment. Instead, he had to pay the debt with his life's work, his most cherished possessions. He had to hand over his entire workshop—including the printing press, all his carefully crafted materials, and the metal type for the Bible and the Psalter. Half the Bibles Gutenberg had already printed went to Fust, too.

Fust lost no time taking advantage of Gutenberg's work. He quickly finished Gutenberg's books. It was easy because he had the perfect partner—Peter Schöffer, Gutenberg's former apprentice. In 1456, Fust and Schöffer officially published Gutenberg's famous Bible. It was the world's first book ever printed with movable type. Fust and Schöffer published Gutenberg's Psalter in 1457.

GUTENBERG'S BIBLE

Gutenberg's Bible is called the Forty-two-Line Bible. It had two columns of type on each page, and each column had forty-two lines of type. The complete Bible had 1,282 pages, which were bound in two volumes. This was a promising beginning. Today the Bible is the most-printed book in the world.

Most Gutenberg Bibles were printed on paper, although some were printed on vellum. It is believed that about 180 copies were made with Gutenberg's equipment from 1454 to 1457. Working by hand, a scribe would have produced only one Bible during that time.

Only forty-eight original Gutenberg Bibles are known to exist today, but not all are complete. Just a few are considered perfect, with no missing pages. One is in the Library of Congress in Washington, D.C. Some others are in the British Library in London, England, and the Bibliotèque Nationale de Paris in France.

Life Goes On

As for Gutenberg, the loss of his workshop was a terrible blow. After years of trial and error, he had watched his creation come to life—a magnificent Bible, printed on his own movable-type press. But he never got to share in the excitement of releasing it to the public. Few people even knew this Bible was his.

Nevertheless, life went on for Gutenberg. He opened another shop and went on printing things that had a ready

Though Gutenberg lost his first workshop, he later opened another that printed schoolbooks, prayerbooks, and calendars.

market—Latin schoolbooks, prayer books, and calendars. Church officials appreciated this work. In 1465, the archbishop of Mainz wrote a letter commending Gutenberg for printing materials so helpful to the Church. He gave Gutenberg the title of courtier, or attendant at the royal court. Along with that came special favors. Once a year Gutenberg received a wardrobe of courtier's clothing. He also got 2,180 liters (576 gallons) of grain and 2,000 liters (528 g) of wine per year.

Now, at least, Gutenberg could enjoy some honor in his community. With his yearly gifts he was able to live comfortably. But he never got to see the earth-shattering effects of his invention, and he never got to enjoy the credit and praise he deserved. He is believed to have died around February 3, 1468.

CHAPTER FOUR

How Did He Do It?

How did Gutenberg develop his printing method? How did he solve each problem and work out each detail? What experiments did he try? What failures did he suffer before he succeeded at last? These are fascinating questions, but we will never know all the answers. Gutenberg worked in secret, and he left no notes behind. But we can still piece together some clues by looking at each element of his printing process. Some things he improved, and others he invented. Some ideas came from crafts that had nothing to do with printing. The genius was in putting them all together.

Molds and Dies

Did you ever bake muffins? If you did, you poured batter into a muffin tin. After baking, the muffins' bottoms were shaped exactly like the hollows in the muffin tin. That muffin tin is a mold. Molds are usually concave—hollowed out or rounded in—like the inside of a bowl. Many factory-made items today are made with molds. Just look at any action figure, toy car, or doll. *Molten* metal or plastic was poured or injected into a mold to make its parts. Even some real car parts, such as bumpers and doors, are made in molds.

How do you make a mold? One way is to take an object you want to reproduce. Then, press it into a soft material such as clay. The clay will be indented with a backwards image of your original object. Pour liquid plaster into that space, and wait until the plaster gets hard and dry. You will end up with a model of the original.

In this example the original object is called a *die*. Some printing guilds were using dies in Gutenberg's time. They made a die for each letter of the alphabet by carving the letter into brass or bronze. To spell out words, they hammered the dies, letter by letter, into a soft material.

Once a whole page was done, they had a mold. It had hollowed-out letters, just like the hollows in that muffin tin. Then they poured molten lead into the mold to make a full-page printing plate with raised letters. Gutenberg himself was printing this way in the 1430s.

Why Not Make the Letters Move?

This method presented some problems. No one could hammer every single letter die with the same force. Some letters pressed more deeply into the mold, while others were not as deep. As a result, the surface of the printing plate was uneven. Some letters printed darkly, while others were light and barely readable. Also, as each die was hammered into the mold, the hammering moved or squashed the letter next to it.

Gutenberg solved these problems. Instead of making a mold for a whole page, he made a mold for each letter of the alphabet. All the molds were exactly the same depth, so all the pieces would print with the same darkness.

Gutenberg poured molten metal into each mold. He ended up with a small block of metal type for each letter. He made almost three hundred characters in all, including capital and small letters,

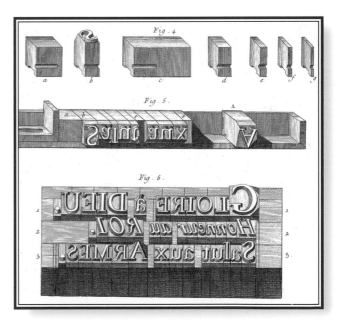

Movable type allowed printers to put individual letters together in a type tray that was then used to print a page of text.

numbers, punctuation marks, and ligatures, or two-letter combinations. There were also "blanks" for spaces. These little metal blocks were Gutenberg's movable type.

TYPESETTERS AND CASES

In the early days of printing, metal type was kept in big cases (below right) that slid out of a cabinet with many drawers. The *typesetter*, or compositor, sat before the type case and picked up the letters one by one. He or she lined them up on a wooden rack called a composing stick (top right). The typesetter spaced the words out so all the lines were the same width.

Each strip of type would become one line of the printed page. After a page's worth of lines were set, they were assembled on a wooden tray called a *galley*. This gave typesetters the nickname "galley slaves."

In printers' terms, capital letters are called uppercase letters. The small letters are called lowercase letters. That's because printers kept capital letters in the upper case of the cabinet and small letters in the lower case. Later, typesetting was done by machine and, eventually, by computer. Nevertheless, the terms "uppercase" and "lowercase" are still used for capital and small letters.

Letters That Last

Before Gutenberg's invention, most printers were still printing with woodblocks. Wood had its drawbacks, though. The raised letters were pressed against paper hundreds of times. Naturally, the surfaces wore down over time. Using lead printing plates saved a lot of time. No one had to sit and carve out a whole page by hand. Lead was much stronger than wood, too. Still, lead had its problems. It was a soft metal and, like wood, it wore out over time.

Gutenberg knew that metal was the material to use to make his type. But which metal? It is very likely that he looked back on his experience making pilgrim mirrors. The mirrors' metal frames were cast from an alloy.

Gutenberg liked lead because it melted fast and cooled quickly. But lead was soft, so he added antimony to it. This element would make the letters of type harder. They would therefore last longer and keep their sharp edges. He also added a bit of tin because it helped keep the lead from breaking down over time. Even today, metal type is made from an alloy of lead, antimony, and tin.

Ink That Won't Run

Watch a raindrop hit a windowpane. It lands and then quickly trickles down the glass. But put a drop of vegetable oil on the same window. It runs down much more slowly than a water drop does. That's because oil is thicker and stickier than water. This gives you an idea of how Gutenberg came up with a good printing ink.

Before Gutenberg's time most printers were using water-based inks. They mixed water with soot—the fine,

Gutenberg's ink was perfect for printing. Unlike water-based ink that ran off the pieces of metal type, his oil-based ink stuck to them

black powder that gathered in chimneys. The problem was that this ink was runny, and it smeared. It soaked through the paper, too. Printers could print on only one side of a page. Gutenberg surely tried water-based ink with his metal type. He would have found that it didn't stick to the type very well.

Gutenberg solved this problem by developing an oil-based ink from linseed oil. He knew that oil was not as runny as water. Oil was slightly sticky, too, so it would stick to metal. But what would he add to produce the color black? Other printers were using soot, but Gutenberg brought in his knowledge of metals. He added copper, lead, and other metals to the oil. Gutenberg's black inks turned out very dark and glossy—almost glittering. Even today, after more than 550 years, the ink in Gutenberg Bibles is still a sharp, shiny black.

FROM EGGS TO LINSEED OIL

Gutenberg may have borrowed the idea of making oil-based ink from the art world. For hundreds of years artists had been painting with egg tempera. That was a water-based paint with egg and color added. However, in Gutenberg's lifetime, artists were beginning to try oil-based paints. They crushed flax seeds to produce linseed oil. When boiled, the oil became thicker. Then they added various substances to create different colors.

Why Not Use a Machine?

Gutenberg wasn't satisfied with the way ink was put onto paper. Workers simply laid the paper against the inked type and rubbed it to make sure it picked up all the inked letters. Gutenberg wanted to make a machine to do what human workers did, and to do it even better. His solution was the screw press. This press used a huge wooden screw to press the printing plate firmly onto the paper.

How does a screw press work? Imagine an enormous screw standing upright. At the top is a wheel or bar. At the bottom of the screw is a large, flat surface. Someone turns the wheel or bar round and round. As it turns, the flat surface moves down toward a level platform. The more turns, the tighter the two surfaces are squeezed together.

In Gutenberg's time people used screw presses for many purposes.

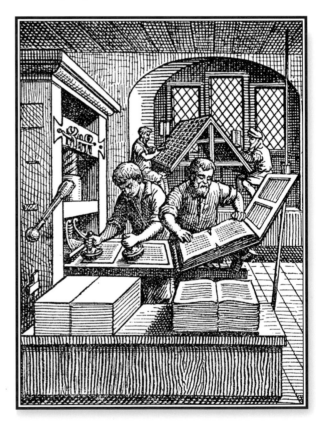

In this sixteenth-century printshop, a worker adjusts paper on the press (right) while the other (left) inks the type.

42

This fifteenth-century painting depicts an apprentice pulling a bar that turns the screw, lowering the platen until it presses paper against the inked letters.

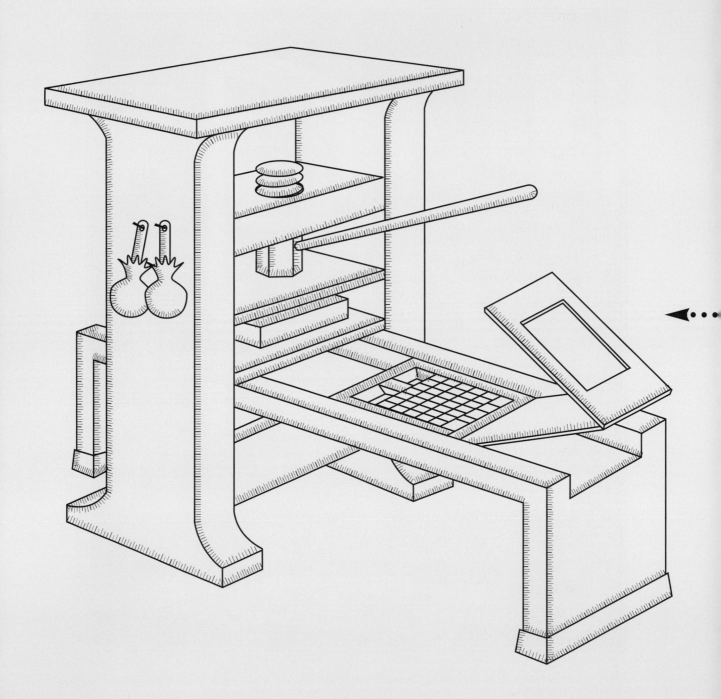

They pressed grapes to make wine, apples to make cider, and olives to get oil. Gutenberg's city of Mainz lay on the Rhine River. All along the river valley, wine makers were pressing their grapes in screw presses. Bookbinders and paper makers were using screw presses, too. As Gutenberg puzzled over how to press paper against the type, the screw press popped into his mind as the perfect solution.

Printing presses followed Gutenberg's basic design for more than three hundred years. Only minor changes were made during that time. For example, the form holding the type was put onto slides or rollers. Then workers could slide it out from under the platen, reload another page's worth of type, and slide it under the platen for printing. A flat wooden paper holder, rather than a person, laid the paper onto the inked type surface.

At last, Gutenberg had all the pieces in place to make his printing press work. Its huge screw stood upright in a wooden frame. At the bottom of the screw was a board called the ***platen***. Beneath all this stood a tabletop. On it lay a full page of metal type held tightly in a frame called a ***form***.

One worker soaked a leather pad in ink and spread the ink onto the type. Another worker placed a moist sheet of paper in a frame between the platen and the form. Next, the press operator pulled a bar to turn the screw. The platen moved lower and lower, pressing the paper firmly against the inked letters. The press operator turned the screw the other way to raise the platen back up.

The printed page was carefully peeled off the form and hung on a rack to dry. This whole process was repeated to make many copies of each page. Once the pages were dry, they could be printed on the reverse side.

Clearly, Gutenberg did not invent his printing press from scratch. He took techniques that already existed, studied each one, and improved them. Best of all, he put them together in a way that no one had thought of before. This added a new element to printing—speed. Books could then be mass-produced.

CHAPTER FIVE

The Information Explosion

Johannes Gutenberg's printing system spread through Europe like wildfire. Nothing could keep it a secret. By 1500, less than fifty years after Gutenberg's invention was completed, there were more than nine million books in print!

Never before had the world seen such an explosion of information. Now, for the first time, ordinary people could read about medicine, science, and astronomy. They could discover a whole new world from geography books and maps. There were books on law, politics, and exploration. There were guides and how-to manuals on farming, metal-working, and using proper manners.

In the early days of printing, Europe had a rather low rate of literacy—the ability to read and write. Traveling readers sometimes read in local marketplaces as a form of entertainment.

But the increased availability of books soon encouraged more and more people to learn to read. Books offered a tantalizing promise of discovery and adventure.

Education for the Masses

It used to take months or even years to produce one hand-copied book. Only wealthy people could afford to buy them.

Reading and learning spread throughout Europe during the fourteenth century as more and more books were printed.

With the introduction of the printing press, it would take only a few days to print the same book. Because much less labor was involved, books could be had for a much lower price than before. Now a whole new class of people could study and learn. No longer was education available only to the wealthy.

Books used to be written in Latin, the language of the church and of scholars. But after 1500, more and more books were printed in the vernacular—the common, spoken language. This opened up worlds of literature to ordinary people. Now they could read books written by the world's great authors in their own language.

Of course, not everyone welcomed the printing press. Many people of the noble classes looked down on printed books. They felt that only hand-lettered books were worth owning. Church leaders welcomed printing at first. It meant that more people could read the Bible and other religious works. Later, though, church officials worried that some books would corrupt people's minds.

In reality, printed books gave people the freedom to think for themselves. They no longer needed authorities to tell them what to think. They could learn information and then use it to choose which opinions to adopt. They could ask questions and challenge old ideas. This allowed new attitudes and ways of thinking. People finally had the power and the tools to develop their own opinions.

Changing Minds: Revolution and Reform

Printing affordable books became a powerful way to change people's minds. Someone with revolutionary new ideas could now spread them around quickly. Take religious beliefs, for example. Until the 1500s Roman Catholicism was Europe's dominant religion. But some bishops and priests were growing dissatisfied with the church's teachings and practices.

In 1517, a German priest named Martin Luther went public with his complaints. He published them in his Ninety-five Theses, a list of arguments condemning church practices he disliked. This marks the beginning of a religious revolution called the Protestant Reformation. Out of this revolution came the founding of Protestantism, which quickly become a major branch of Christianity.

Printed copies of the Ninety-five Theses spread across Germany and northern Europe, exposing thousands of people to Luther's views. He went on to publish hundreds of pamphlets and sermons. He even printed a translation of the Bible in the German language.

John Calvin was another Protestant reformer. He first published his teachings in 1536. Thanks to the printing press, they spread into France, England, and many other countries. By the mid-1500s, much of Europe had converted to Protestantism.

THE FRANKFURT BOOK FAIR

Many European cities held annual fairs. They were like today's trade shows, art fairs, or county fairs. They were big markets where merchants set up booths. Shoppers came from faraway cities to check out the latest products.

The city of Frankfurt, Germany, held its first book fair in 1480. Booksellers, book collectors, and other interested people came to buy books for their shops and libraries back home. The Frankfurt Book Fair was a major cultural event in Europe until it declined in the early 1900s. It began again in 1949.

Today the Frankfurt Book Fair is the largest book fair in the world. Thousands of publishers from all over the world come to exhibit their books. Many deals are made there. For example, a publisher might buy the right to publish a foreign book in his or her own language. The fair is a great way to spread ideas and literature around the world, just as it was in 1480.

Is It Eggs or Eyren?

Have you ever spelled a word incorrectly? That spelling might have been acceptable at one time. In the 1400s, people in different regions of a country spoke different dialects, or versions, of their language. Their spellings of words varied, too. Printers often wondered which version of a word to print in a book.

The English printer William Caxton faced this problem. "Lo! what should a man in these days now write," he moaned— "eggs or eyren?" Caxton chose spellings that were understood by the most people. This helped shape the English language into its present form, with standard spellings. The same thing happened in Germany, France, Italy, and other countries.

Printed books forced information to be more accurate, too. Before, scribes might make mistakes when copying books. There were even scribes who could write well but couldn't read! They could easily make errors that were then copied by other scribes. An author might even be tempted to write something false. Now, however, book owners could assemble many books on the same subject. They could easily check facts by comparing one book to another.

Human Rights and Freedom of the Press

The ancient Greeks wrote about natural laws. These are rights and duties that all humans have, just for being alive. By the 1700s, this idea had expanded. Philosophers began to talk about basic human rights. This became the basis for the United States's Declaration of Independence. All people, it said, have the right to "Life, Liberty, and the Pursuit of Happiness."

CENSORSHIP: WORDS ON FIRE

Throughout history, various groups have censored, or banned, books. In 1559, for example, the Roman Catholic Church began publishing a list called the Index of Forbidden Books. It would include writings by the astronomer Nicholaus Copernicus. He put forth the idea that Earth revolves around the sun. At the time this was seen as contrary to the Bible's teachings.

Censorship is often a tool used by non-democratic governments. They hope to suppress ideas that threaten their authority. In Nazi Germany Adolf Hitler ordered massive book burnings in the 1930s. Huge bonfires consumed tens of thousands of books.

China launched a Cultural Revolution in 1966. It aimed to destroy all anti-communist thought, especially religious ideas. Chinese soldiers burned entire libraries of handwritten books in Tibet's Buddhist monasteries. The former Soviet Union censored not only books and newspapers but also radio and television broadcasts.

Salman Rushdie, a British writer from India, learned that censorship can be deadly. In 1988, he published *The Satanic Verses*. It was a fictional novel about Muhammad, the founder of Islam. An Islamic leader offended by the book then issued a death order against Rushdie, who went into hiding. Only in 1998 was the order lifted.

Schools and libraries sometimes ban books they consider to be unfit for young people. Mark Twain's books *Tom Sawyer* and *Huckleberry Finn* have been banned from time to time. The complaint is that they portray a negative view of African Americans.

The Founding Fathers also added a Bill of Rights to the U.S. Constitution. The very first item in the Bill of Rights, the First Amendment, guarantees freedom of the press. That means the freedom to print, distribute, and read almost anything at all.

The United States has led the way in granting freedom of the press to citizens through the First Amendment.

Of course, the ancient Greeks would never have thought of the right to freedom of the press. They had no printing presses. But freedom of the press is now considered a basic human right worldwide. It is a cornerstone of any democratic society. Imagine how Gutenberg would have felt. His invention, the printing press, would stand for freedom itself!

Still, most democratic countries have laws against printing certain materials. One example is called libel. Libel is publishing things that hurt someone's reputation. Many cities, states, and countries also have laws against printing indecent material. The interpretation of these laws often leads to heated arguments in courts.

CHAPTER SIX

From Hot Type to Cyberspace

Gutenberg's system of printing was a good one. Printers used his method for more than three hundred years. During that time only small changes were made in the printing process. Around 1500, for example, printers replaced the wooden screw with an iron screw. The form holding the type was put onto slides or rollers. Then workers could slide it out from under the platen, reload another form of type, and slide it under the platen for printing. A flat, wooden paper holder, rather than a person, laid the paper onto the inked type surface.

Around 1790, the British scientist William Nicholson improved the inking process. Until this time workers dabbed ink onto the type with leather sponges. Nicholson took a leather-covered *cylinder*, inked it, and rolled it across the

Ink-covered rollers improved the printing process by eliminating the need to dab ink onto the type by hand.

type. If you've ever seen house painters use paint rollers, you can picture how the cylinder worked.

Replacing Gutenberg's famous screw was a landmark in printing-press history. The British earl Charles Stanhope took the first step in that direction. He designed an all-iron press around 1800. Its iron levers added tremendous power to the screw.

It was only a matter of time until presses used levers to replace the screw itself. One example was a small press

Charles Stanhope's all-iron printing press was able to push the paper against the type with tremendous pressure.

called the **platen jobber**, or jobbing platen. Printers used it to print small jobs, such as posters and business cards. The platen and the type surface opened and shut on a hinge, like two huge jaws.

All the News of the Day

Newspaper publishers drove the next inventions. They needed to print lots of papers fast. Hand-operated presses just couldn't work fast enough. In the early 1800s, Friedrich

Friedrich Koening improved upon the printing press by building a steam-driven machine that printed more than a thousand pages per hour.

Koenig of Germany figured out how to meet this need. He built a printing press powered by a steam engine. Koenig also changed the way the paper contacted the type.

Until this time, flat sheets of paper were fed into the press one by one. This is called **sheet-fed printing**, and it is still used for small printing jobs. Koenig decided to wrap the paper around a cylinder. It rolled across the type like a rolling pin. The *Times* of London first used Koenig's steam-powered cylinder press in 1814. It could print more than a thousand pages an hour.

Other newspapers quickly adopted these innovations. As a result, newspapers became cheaper. By 1833, Benjamin Day of the *New York Sun* could sell his papers for a penny a copy. He was delighted that he could now "lay before the public, at a price well within the means of everyone, all the news of the day."

Rollers and More Rollers

Until this point, printing was done on a **flatbed press.** The type lay flat while paper was pressed or rolled onto it. Richard March Hoe changed that. He put the type itself onto a cylinder. The type cylinder picked up ink from the ink cylinder, and the ink-covered type rolled against the paper. This is now called a **rotary press**.

Hoe's press had some problems at first. The type was clamped tightly around the cylinder, but not tightly enough.

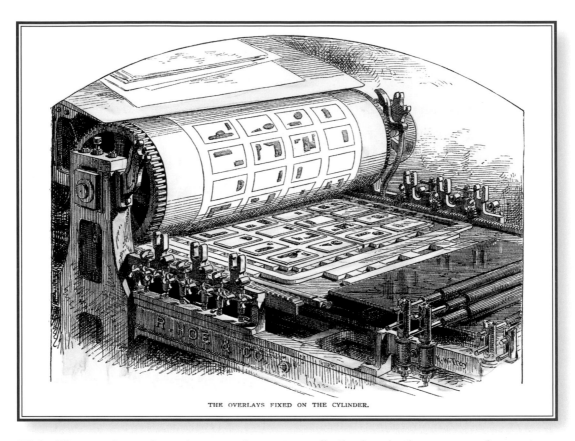

THE OVERLAYS FIXED ON THE CYLINDER.

This illustration of a nineteenth-century flatbed printing press shows type locked on the bed and paper fixed on the cylinder.

Pieces of type kept falling out. This, too, had a solution. The type was pressed into a soft material to make a mold. Then, molten lead was poured into the mold to make a one-piece printing plate. That plate was fastened to the cylinder.

The rotary press was great for printing newspapers. The *Philadelphia Public Ledger* first used it in 1847. It could print eight thousand pages an hour. It is no wonder that Hoe's invention was called the "lightning press."

Someone still had to attach each sheet of paper to the paper cylinder. William Bullock thought this took too much time. In 1865, he invented a printing press that used a continuous roll of paper. The paper wove up, down, around, and through the printing press. It reminded people of a spider weaving in and out as it spins it web, so it was called a **web press**. On its way through the web, the paper got printed on both sides and then cut.

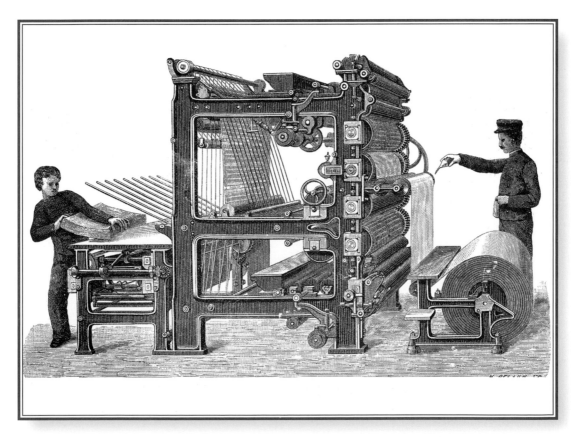

In the mid-1860s, the web press was introduced. Paper was fed from a continuous roll through the printer, printing type on both sides.

TYPESETTING SPEEDS UP

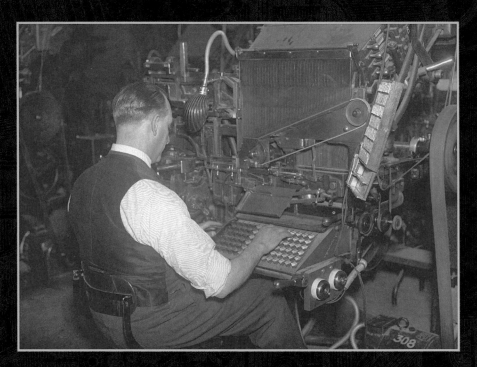

In 1884, Ottmar Mergenthaler of Germany invented the Linotype. This was a mechanical typesetting machine. Until that point, human typesetters reached for each letter and lined them up by hand. Now they typed the letters at a keyboard, and a machine put them in place. This was a big leap forward in speed.

The Linotype machine set an entire line of type at a time and cast it into a solid piece of metal. A slightly later invention, the Monotype, set the characters one by one. This was useful in cases where one page or one line contained different kinds of characters—boldface type, italic type, mathematical symbols, and so on.

Offset Printing

The next important invention solved a serious problem. Printing plates took a real beating. They rolled against the paper with a lot of pressure, and the images on their surface wore off quickly. In 1903, the American printer Ira Rubel thought of a way to save the printing plates.

First, he applied ink to the type on the printing cylinder. Then, he rolled the inked cylinder against a smooth rubber roller, which picked up the inked image. This rubber cylinder was then rolled across the paper, leaving the inked image on the paper. In this method the type never even touches the paper. Instead, the inked image is offset, or set off, by an intermediate roller. This is called *offset printing*. Today, offset presses print newspapers, magazines, books, and other high-volume printing jobs.

Hot Type Goes Cold

For almost five hundred years, molten metal was cast to make pieces of type, and later, printing plates. This is called the *hot type* method. Around 1950, *phototypesetting* changed all that. In this process the text was typed and printed on high-quality paper. Then it was photographed, producing a sheet of film. That film was used to make a printing plate. No metal was melted and cast at all. The days of hot type were over. *Cold type* had arrived.

In the 1960s, computers created a worldwide revolution in science and technology. Naturally, computers changed the printing industry, too. Electronic typesetting and book production became the standard. By the 1980s, *desktop publishing* was replacing older methods of composition that required huge machines and many human tasks. Those functions could take place by computer on someone's desktop.

Now an author submits an electronic file to a publisher. Editing and page layout all take place on computers. Both

A designer can lay out the cover of a book using desktop publishing technology.

words and pictures are set in place. Then, an entire book or magazine is downloaded onto a computer disk and given to a printer. In contrast, imagine what a bulky production Gutenberg's Bible was. Just one page worth of metal type weighed several pounds!

Books in the Information Age

Computer networks and the Internet ushered in the information age. These inventions were as revolutionary as the printing press. They enabled people to spread information to millions of readers through cyberspace with lightning speed. Imagine how surprised Gutenberg would have been—the words never reached paper at all!

A new kind of book arrived on the scene—the e-book. That's a book published online meant for reading on a computer screen instead of on a printed page. Hundreds of online magazines, or e-zines, also sprang up. New technologies could compress information into a tiny space, too. An entire set of encyclopedias can fit onto one compact disc (CD). Readers just pop it into a computer to look things up.

The dawn of the information age inspired many gloomy predictions. Printed books would be phased out, some people said. They would become out-of-date, antiques, or relics of the past. Most book lovers disagree. They say printed books will never die. They like the feel and smell of a book. They like turning the pages. And there's nothing like

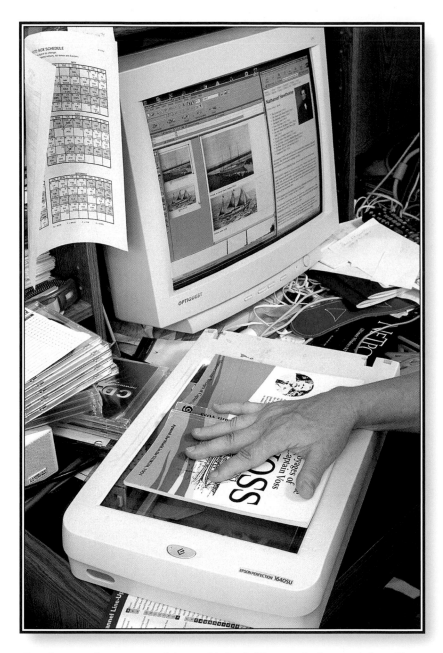

Books can be scanned into digital files and then read online
via a computer.

The printed word has the power to educate, motivate, and captivate!

curling up in a cozy corner or under a tree with a good book. Curling up with a computer? Well . . . it's just not the same!

The printing industry has seen many changes since Johannes Gutenberg's time. But one thing has stayed the same for more than five hundred years. The most important aspect of printing is not the technology. Now, as always, we treasure printing for the ideas passed on through the printed word.

The Printing Press: A Timeline

Chinese court official Ts'ai Lun invents paper. *p. 17*

Johannes Gutenberg prints the first copies of his forty-two-line Bible on his movable-type printing press; he loses his printing operation to Johann Fust. *p. 31*

Fust and Schöffer publish Gutenberg's Psalter, the first example of color printing. *p. 32*

William Nicholson begins applying ink to the type with a cylinder. *p. 55*

A.D. 105	About c.1041	1455	1456	1457	About c.1500	About c.1790	About c.1800

Chinese inventor Pi Sheng makes movable type from clay. *p. 13*

Johann Fust and Peter Schöffer publish Gutenberg's Bible. *pp. 31–32*

Printers replace the wood screw with an iron screw. *p. 55*

The British earl Charles Stanhope builds the first all-iron printing press. *p. 57*

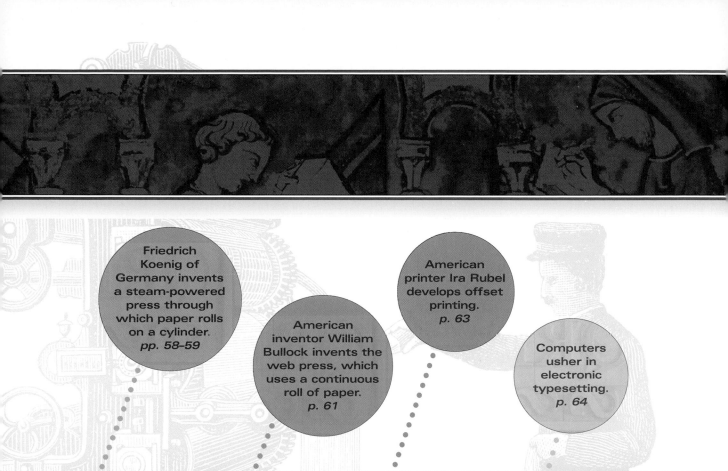

Friedrich Koenig of Germany invents a steam-powered press through which paper rolls on a cylinder.
pp. 58–59

American inventor William Bullock invents the web press, which uses a continuous roll of paper.
p. 61

American printer Ira Rubel develops offset printing.
p. 63

Computers usher in electronic typesetting.
p. 64

About 1814   1847   1865   1884   1903   c. 1950   1960s   1980s

American inventor Richard March Hoe patents the first rotary printing press, which puts the printing plate on a cylinder.
p. 59

Ottmar Mergenthaler of Germany invents the Linotype, a mechanical typesetting machine.
p. 62

Photographic film is used to make printing plates.
p. 63

With desktop publishing, many typesetting and printing tasks take place on desktop computers.
p. 64

69

Glossary

alloy: a substance made of a combination of different metals

apprentices: young people studying with a master craftsperson to learn a specialized craft or trade

cold type: printing plates made from photographic film

cylinder: an object with a curved surface, like a tube or a rolling pin

desktop publishing: production of printed material on a desktop computer; may involve typesetting, page layout, and inserting pictures

die: an object used to indent a mold for reproducing many copies of that object; sometimes the term is used to refer to the mold itself

flatbed press: a printing press in which the type rests on a flat surface *form:* a frame that holds a page of type together tightly for printing

galley: a tray that tightly holds a column or page of typeset text; also, a sheet of paper printed from that tray for purposes of editing or proofreading

guilds: associations of artisans and craft workers devoted to the quality production of specialized craft items

hot type: pieces of type or printing plates cast from molten metal

journeyman: a worker who has learned a craft from a master and is allowed to work for wages

mold: a hollowed-out frame into which a liquid is poured so it will harden in a certain shape

molten: melted; refers especially to metals

movable type: type in which the letters and other characters are separate pieces of metal that are assembled to create a text

offset printing: printing method in which a rubber cylinder rolls against the printing plate, picks up the inked image, and rolls the image onto the paper

parchment: an animal skin cleaned, stretched, and scraped to be suitable as a writing surface; usually sheep, goat, or calf skin

phototypesetting: typesetting by keyboard to produce text on photographic film from which printing plates are made; also called photocomposition

platen: on early printing presses, a flat plate that was lowered by the turn of a screw to press paper against the type

platen jobber: a printing press in which the platen and the type surface open and shut on a hinge

pulp: wood or other materials reduced to a soft mass, often by chopping, beating, or boiling

rotary press: a printing press in which the type is wrapped around a revolving cylinder

sheet-fed printing: printing on single sheets of paper

typesetter: also called compositor; originally, a person who set pieces of movable type into place by hand; later, a person who operates mechanical or computer typesetting equipment

vellum: a fine-quality parchment made from the delicate skin of young animals

web press: a printing press that prints on a continuous roll of paper

To Find Out More

Books

Brookfield, Karen, and Laurence Pordes (illustrator). *Book*. New York: DK, 2000.

Burch, Joann Johansen, and Kent Alan Aldrich (illustrator). *Fine Print: A Story About Johann Gutenberg*. Minneapolis: Carolrhoda, 1991.

Crompton, Samuel Willard. *The Printing Press*. Philadelphia: Chelsea House, 2003.

Graham, Ian A. *Books and Newspapers*. Austin, TX: Raintree Steck-Vaughn, 2000.

Koscielniak, Bruce. *Johann Gutenberg and the Amazing Printing Press*. Boston: Houghton Mifflin, 2003.

Meltzer, Milton. *The Printing Press*. New York: Benchmark Books, 2003.

Pollard, Michael, and Anna Sproule. *Johann Gutenberg: Master of Modern Printing*. Woodbridge, CT: Blackbirch Press, 2001.

Tames, Richard. *The Printing Press: A Breakthrough in Communication*. Chicago: Heinemann Library, 2001.

Web Sites

Gutenberg and His Impact

http://www.gutenbergdigital.de/gudi/start.htm

This Web site contains extensive information on Gutenberg's life and achievements.

Printing: History and Development

http://www.karmak.org/archive/2002/08/history_of_print.html

A site that examines the history of printing from its earliest times through the modern age.

From Pen to Printing Press

http://www.beyondbooks.com/leu11/2e.asp

This is an entertaining look at the history of writing and printing.

The Printers Guild

http://www.twingroves.district96.k12.il.us/Renaissance/guildhall/printer/printingguild.html

This Web site explores the printing process from the viewpoint of an apprentice.

Organizations

The Museum of Printing History
1324 West Clay
Houston, TX 77019
713-522-4652

The Museum of Printing
800 Massachusetts Avenue
North Andover, MA 01845
978-686-0450
www.museumofprinting.org

The International Printing Museum
315 Torrance Boulevard
Carson, CA 90745
310-515-7166 (museum)
www.printmuseum.org

The American Printing History Association
P.O. Box 4519
Grand Central Station
New York, NY 10163
www.printinghistory.org

Index

About the Author

Ann Heinrichs used to spend summer afternoons in her grandfather's basement. There, on a creaky, oily printing press, he printed advertising handbills, using tweezers to set the type. It was only natural that Ann was drawn to the publishing industry. Over time she moved from print production manager to editor to advertising copywriter to book author. Along the way she got to know the inner workings of print shops, pressrooms, and binderies.

All these experiences helped her with writing this book. In addition, Ann read current biographies of Gutenberg and explored Internet sites detailing scientific studies of his work. She also examined illuminated manuscripts such as the *Book of Kells* in Ireland and early Bible texts in Greece.

Ann grew up in Fort Smith, Arkansas, and holds a bachelor's and master's degree in piano performance. She has written more than one hundred books for children and young adults on U.S. and world history and culture.

80